A Zondervan/Ladybird Bible Book

Jesus in Danger

By Jenny Robertson
Illustrated by Alan Parry

Z ZONDERVAN PUBLISHING HOUSE
OF THE ZONDERVAN CORPORATION
GRAND RAPIDS, MICHIGAN 49506

Jerusalem's high towers shone in the spring sun. Great danger lay in wait for Jesus. The chief priests, who hated Him, planned to kill Him. Jesus knew all about the danger, but He knew, too, that it was God's plan for Him to die and come to life again.

As they made their way toward the city, Jesus said to two of His friends, "Our holy writings say that the King God is sending will ride into Jerusalem on a donkey. In that village over there you will find a young donkey. Untie him and bring him to Me. If anyone complains, say that the Master needs him."

They found the donkey easily, and started to untie him. "Hey! Stop!" A man poked his head around the doorway. "What are you doing, taking that donkey?"

"The Master needs it!" said the friends, as Jesus had told them. "Oh, well, that's different!" said the man. "Of course you can take the donkey. Treat him carefully, won't you—no one has ever ridden him before." They untied the donkey and led him to Jesus.

Crowds of people were flocking to Jerusalem for the Passover Festival. Everybody was happy because of the holiday. When they saw Jesus, they cheered with excitement. "Here comes God's King!" they shouted. People waved green branches, and spread their cloaks in front of the donkey, as he carried Jesus slowly into the city and through the streets to the temple, where people gathered to praise God.

The Temple court was like a huge, noisy marketplace where people could buy animals and birds to offer to God. Lambs bleated loudly while doves cooed in cages. Special coins had to be used inside the temple, so everyone had to change his money just as though he were going to a foreign country. The moneychangers were cheats and kept some of the change. "You've made God's temple like a robbers' den!" Jesus said. "Get out!" He toppled over their tables. Coins rolled in all directions.

The temple was in an uproar! Doves flew free from their cages with a flapping of wings. The dealers shouted and raged as Jesus drove them out. Sheep butted each other; calves lowed. The priests were furious.

Every day that week Jesus went back to the temple. The priests tried to trap Him with trick questions. "Teacher," they said politely, "should we pay taxes to the Romans, or not?"

Jesus saw through the trick at once. "Let Me see a coin. Whose name and head are stamped on it?" He asked them.

"The Roman emperor's," they replied.

"Then pay the Roman emperor what is his, and pay God what belongs to Him," answered Jesus. Silenced, they slunk away, but Jesus knew that they still watched Him closely.

Jesus and His friends watched rich people dropping silver coins into the collecting boxes in the temple. They noticed a very poor woman, who was weak and feeble. She was a widow, with no husband to help her. She dropped two small copper coins into the box.

"Look, friends," said Jesus. "This poor woman has put in far more than all the rich people we have seen."

"Has she?" said His friends, amazed.

"Yes," Jesus answered. "You see, they gave God only what they thought they could spare. They have plenty of money left, but she is so poor she had only those two coins. She has given God all the money she had."

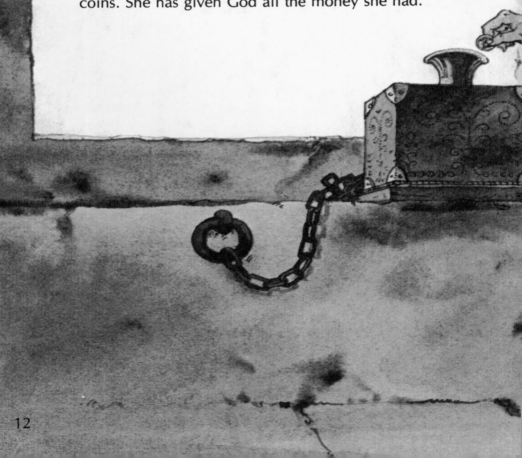

13

One evening, a woman named Mary poured expensive perfume over Jesus' hair and feet. A wonderful scent filled the room. Mary's tears fell on Jesus' feet as she kissed them and wiped them with her hair.

"What a waste!" said Judas. "Mary could have sold this perfume and given the money to poor people."

"No," said Jesus. "Mary has done a beautiful thing for Me before I die." Mary was glad, but Judas scowled angrily at Jesus' words.

Judas looked after the money for Jesus and the others, and he used to help himself from what was there. If Mary had sold her perfume, there would have been more money for him to steal. Now every day he grew greedier for money, and he began to be angry with Jesus because Jesus cared for different things. At last Judas went to the priests.

"What will you give me if I help you capture Jesus?" he asked. They counted thirty silver coins into his hand. Judas slipped away, but he was watchful now, waiting for a time when Jesus was alone and His enemies could capture Him without any trouble.

Jesus and His friends ate the festival meal in a secret room in Jerusalem. They had special bread, and lamb with sauce and herbs. Jesus spoke to them about the love of God. Then He took off His long tunic and tied a towel around His waist. He poured water into a bowl and, just like a servant, washed the dusty feet of his friends. Simon Peter said, "Lord, You mustn't wash my feet as if You were a servant!"

"I'm washing your feet because I love you," said Jesus. "You must be ready, too, to serve one another in humble ways."

Jesus sat down again. "One of you is going to hand Me over to My enemies," He said.

Who could it be?" they wondered anxiously, but Judas knew. Quietly he slipped outside.

Then Jesus took some bread, broke it, and shared it with His friends. "This is my body," He said. "When you break and eat bread together like this, you must remember Me."

Sad and puzzled, they shared the bread.

Then Jesus passed the cup of wine around to them. "Drink this, all of you," He said. "This is my blood, which will be poured out so that people's sins can be forgiven by God."

They did not understand. Why did He talk about dying when every day crowds followed Him and praised Him? Sadly, they went with Him out to a quiet garden.

On their way, Jesus warned them again of all that was to happen. "I'll stick by you," declared Simon Peter, "even if all the others run away and leave you."

"Before you hear the rooster crow tomorrow morning, you will say three times that you do not know Me," said Jesus. "Pray for Me," He added. Then He went on and prayed alone, "Father, if it is possible, don't let Me go through this terrible death!"

His hair stuck to His forehead, wet with sweat. With a great effort He cried out, "Father, don't do what I want. Do what You know is best."

He returned to His friends and found them asleep. "Could you not stay awake?" asked Jesus. "Get up now. Here come My enemies."

Into the quiet garden came Judas, followed by soldiers and a rough crowd armed with sticks and spears. The chief priests had sent them all to capture Jesus.

"The man I kiss is the one you want," muttered Judas. He went straight to Jesus. "Peace, Teacher," Judas said, and kissed Him.

Jesus looked steadily at Judas. "Why are you here, friend?" He asked gently. "Have you come to give me away with your kiss?" Then the soldiers grabbed Jesus and held Him securely.

"Don't hurt My friends," Jesus warned them.

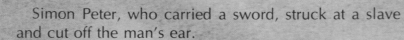

Simon Peter, who carried a sword, struck at a slave and cut off the man's ear.

"Put your sword away, Simon," said Jesus. "I shall go with them willingly, for this is the way My Father has chosen for Me." The crowd grew silent. "Did you have to come with sticks and spears to capture Me?" Jesus asked them. "Day after day I went to the temple. You all saw Me there, but none of you arrested Me then."

He touched the wounded man and healed his ear. "Now is the time for the powers of darkness to have their way," Jesus said. The soldiers hurried Him roughly out of the garden. His terrified friends scattered among the trees, leaving Jesus alone in the power of the men who hated Him and wanted to kill Him.

What happened next?

That was not the end of the story. You can find out what happened after Jesus was arrested by looking in your Bible at Luke chapter 22, verse 54 and reading on to the end of the Gospel.

All the events of this story took place when Jesus was in Jerusalem for the Passover Festival. At Passover time the Jews remembered how God helped their ancestors to escape from Egypt when they were slaves.

You can read about this in your Bible in Exodus chapter 12, verses 15 to 42.

On the night when the slaves escaped from Egypt, God told them to prepare a special meal. Everybody ate roast lamb or goat with flat, "unleavened" bread (leaven is any substance like yeast which is used to make dough rise). Jewish families still eat a special meal together at Passover time, just as the slaves did, and just as Jesus and His friends did. Great care is taken that no food with leaven in it is eaten. No such food is even kept in the house during this time.